Mastering Food Pro

the World o

Nilsson

Copyright © [2023]

Title: Mastering Food Product Design A Journey into the World of Food Engineering

Author's: Nilsson.

This book was printed and published by [Publisher's: Nilsson] in [2023]

ISBN:

TABLE OF CONTENTS

Chapter 5: Food Packaging and Preservation

Packaging Materials and Technologies

Shelf-Life Extension Techniques

Packaging Design and Consumer Appeal

Chapter 6: Food Quality and Safety

Quality Parameters and Assessment Methods

Food Safety Regulations and Compliance

Food Traceability and Supply Chain Management

Chapter 7: Sensory Evaluation and Consumer Testing

Sensory Perception and Evaluation Techniques

Consumer Testing and Market Research

Incorporating Feedback into Food Product Design

Chapter 8: Novel Food Product Design

Functional Foods and Nutraceuticals

Plant-Based and Alternative Protein Products

Sustainable and Eco-Friendly Food Innovations

Chapter 9: Scaling up and Commercialization

Pilot Plant Operations and Scale-Up Considerations

Cost Analysis and Economic Feasibility

Manufacturing Process Optimization

Chapter 1: Introduction to Food Engineering

The Role of Food Engineering in Food Product Design

Food engineering plays a crucial role in the design and development of food products. It encompasses various disciplines, including chemical engineering, to create innovative and safe food products that cater to the ever-changing needs and preferences of consumers. This subchapter aims to explore the importance of food engineering in food product design, with a specific focus on the niche of chemical engineering.

Food engineering involves the application of engineering principles and techniques to the production, processing, and preservation of food. It encompasses a wide range of activities, such as ingredient selection, formulation development, process optimization, and packaging design. Chemical engineering, in particular, plays a significant role in food product design as it focuses on the transformation of raw materials into finished products through chemical processes.

Chemical engineers are responsible for understanding the molecular composition of food ingredients and their interactions during processing. They apply their knowledge to develop efficient and sustainable processes that ensure the safety, quality, and nutritional value of food products. By utilizing their expertise, chemical engineers can enhance the taste, texture, appearance, and shelf life of food products.

One of the key contributions of chemical engineering in food product design is the development of novel food ingredients and additives. These additives can improve the sensory attributes of food products, enhance their nutritional value, and extend their shelf life. Chemical engineers also play a vital role in optimizing processing conditions to ensure the preservation of essential nutrients and the elimination of harmful microorganisms.

Furthermore, chemical engineering principles are instrumental in designing food packaging materials that maintain product integrity and extend shelf life. Chemical engineers work towards developing sustainable packaging solutions that minimize environmental impact while ensuring product safety and quality.

In conclusion, food engineering, with a specific focus on chemical engineering, plays a pivotal role in food product design. It is essential for creating innovative and safe food products that meet the ever-evolving demands of consumers. Chemical engineers contribute to the development of novel ingredients, optimization of processing conditions, and the design of sustainable packaging solutions. By merging engineering principles with the intricacies of food science, food engineers can shape the future of the food industry, improving the quality, safety, and sustainability of the products we consume.

Overview of Food Engineering Principles

Food engineering is a multidisciplinary field that combines principles from various sciences to design and develop safe, nutritious, and high-quality food products. In this subchapter, we will delve into the fundamental principles of food engineering and explore the crucial role it plays in the world of food product design.

Food engineering encompasses knowledge and expertise from several areas, including chemical engineering. Chemical engineering principles are applied to various aspects of food production, such as optimizing the manufacturing process, improving product quality and safety, and developing innovative food products.

One of the key principles in food engineering is understanding the physical and chemical properties of food components. Chemical engineers analyze the composition and interactions of different ingredients to determine optimal processing conditions that preserve the nutritional value and sensory characteristics of the final product. They also study the behavior of food materials under different environmental conditions, such as temperature, pressure, and pH, to ensure stability and shelf-life.

Another important aspect of food engineering is process design and optimization. Chemical engineers utilize their expertise in mass and energy transfer, reaction kinetics, and process modeling to develop efficient and cost-effective manufacturing processes. They aim to minimize waste, reduce energy consumption, and enhance productivity while maintaining the desired product attributes.

Food safety is a critical concern in the food industry, and food engineers play a vital role in ensuring the production of safe and hygienic food products. They apply principles of food microbiology and engineering to develop and implement effective sanitation and sterilization methods, as well as design equipment and packaging systems that prevent contamination and maintain product integrity.

Furthermore, food engineers are at the forefront of innovation in the food industry. They work on developing novel food products, such as functional foods and alternative protein sources, by utilizing advanced technologies and innovative processing techniques. Chemical engineers contribute to these efforts by applying their knowledge of molecular interactions, biochemical reactions, and materials science to create sustainable and healthy food options.

In conclusion, food engineering principles, including those from chemical engineering, are essential for the design and development of safe, nutritious, and innovative food products. By understanding the physical and chemical properties of food components, optimizing manufacturing processes, ensuring food safety, and driving innovation, food engineers contribute significantly to the advancement of the food industry. Whether you are a student of chemical engineering or simply interested in the world of food, understanding these principles will provide you with valuable insights into the fascinating field of food engineering.

Chapter 2: Fundamentals of Food Engineering

Principles of Chemical Engineering in Food Processing

Food processing is a complex and intricate industry that requires a deep understanding of various scientific disciplines. One such discipline that plays a crucial role in the field is chemical engineering. In this subchapter, we will explore the principles of chemical engineering and its applications in food processing.

Chemical engineering is the branch of engineering that combines the principles of chemistry, physics, and mathematics to design, analyze, and improve processes involving the conversion of raw materials into valuable products. In the context of food processing, chemical engineering techniques are employed to optimize the production, quality, and safety of food products.

One key principle of chemical engineering in the food industry is mass balance. This principle involves the careful calculation and control of mass flows throughout the various stages of food processing. By ensuring that the input and output of raw materials, ingredients, and by-products are accurately measured and controlled, chemical engineers can optimize production efficiency and minimize waste.

Another important principle is heat transfer. Chemical engineers use their knowledge of heat transfer mechanisms to design and optimize food processing equipment such as heat exchangers, evaporators, and ovens. By effectively transferring heat, these engineers can ensure that food products are cooked, pasteurized, or sterilized to the required temperature for both safety and quality purposes.

Chemical engineers also play a critical role in the field of food safety. They apply principles of microbiology and biochemistry to develop and implement effective sanitation and hygiene practices in food processing plants. Through their expertise, they can design and implement processes that prevent the growth of harmful microorganisms and ensure the safety of the final food products.

Furthermore, chemical engineering principles are employed in the development of food packaging materials. Chemical engineers work to design packaging materials that provide the necessary barrier properties, such as oxygen and moisture resistance, to preserve the quality and extend the shelf life of food products. They also ensure that the packaging materials are safe and comply with regulatory standards.

In conclusion, chemical engineering principles play a vital role in the field of food processing. From mass balance to heat transfer, food safety to packaging, chemical engineers bring their expertise to optimize production efficiency, ensure food safety, and improve the overall quality of food products. By mastering the principles of chemical engineering in food processing, professionals in the field can contribute to the development of innovative and sustainable solutions that meet the demands of a growing population while ensuring a safe and nutritious food supply for all.

Heat and Mass Transfer in Food Engineering

In the fascinating world of food engineering, the study of heat and mass transfer plays a crucial role in understanding the intricate processes that occur during food production, processing, and preservation. This subchapter aims to provide a comprehensive overview of heat and mass transfer principles as they apply to the field of food engineering, catering to a wide audience including students, professionals, and enthusiasts, particularly those with a background or interest in chemical engineering.

Heat transfer is the process by which thermal energy is transferred from one object or substance to another. In food engineering, this concept is vital in various stages of food processing, such as cooking, baking, and pasteurization. Understanding heat transfer mechanisms, such as conduction, convection, and radiation, allows engineers to optimize processing conditions, ensuring food safety and quality.

Similarly, mass transfer refers to the movement of molecules or substances from one location to another. In food engineering, this process is crucial in areas such as drying, dehydration, and packaging. By comprehending the principles of mass transfer, engineers can design efficient techniques to remove moisture from food products, extend their shelf life, and preserve their sensory properties.

This subchapter delves into the fundamental principles of heat and mass transfer, exploring topics like Fourier's Law, Newton's Law of Cooling, and Fick's Laws of Diffusion. It also discusses the different heat exchangers commonly used in the food industry, such as plate heat exchangers and shell-and-tube heat exchangers, emphasizing their applications and advantages in food processing.

Furthermore, the subchapter covers advanced topics like heat and mass transfer modeling, computational fluid dynamics (CFD), and the use of mathematical equations to predict and optimize heat and mass transfer rates. These concepts are particularly relevant to chemical engineering students and professionals seeking to enhance their understanding of food engineering processes.

By mastering the principles of heat and mass transfer in food engineering, professionals can design innovative food products, improve processing techniques, and enhance food safety and quality. This subchapter serves as a valuable resource for anyone interested in the fascinating and ever-evolving field of food engineering, particularly those with a background in chemical engineering. Whether you are a student embarking on a food engineering journey or a seasoned professional seeking to expand your knowledge, this subchapter will provide you with the necessary foundation to excel in the field.

Fluid Mechanics and Rheology in Food Processing

In the world of food engineering, the principles of fluid mechanics and rheology play a critical role in ensuring the successful design and optimization of food processing operations. Understanding the behavior of fluids and the flow characteristics of food products is essential for achieving desired quality, texture, and shelf life of food products. This subchapter aims to delve into the fascinating realm of fluid mechanics and rheology in food processing, providing insights into various concepts and their applications.

Fluid mechanics is the study of how fluids, such as liquids and gases, behave under different conditions. It encompasses aspects such as fluid flow, fluid properties, and fluid forces. In the context of food processing, fluid mechanics helps engineers understand the movement and distribution of fluids within processing equipment, such as pumps, pipes, and heat exchangers. By analyzing the flow patterns and pressure drops, engineers can optimize the design and layout of processing systems to ensure efficient and cost-effective operations.

Rheology, on the other hand, focuses on the deformation and flow behavior of materials, particularly non-Newtonian fluids like food products. Food products exhibit complex rheological properties due to their composition, which includes various ingredients such as proteins, carbohydrates, and fats. Rheological measurements, such as viscosity, yield stress, and viscoelasticity, provide valuable information for food engineers to optimize processing conditions, such as mixing, pumping, and filling. Understanding the rheological properties of food products is crucial for achieving desired texture, mouthfeel, and sensory attributes.

This subchapter will explore fundamental concepts of fluid mechanics and rheology, including flow behavior classification, viscosity models, and rheological tests commonly used in food engineering. It will also discuss the applications of these concepts in different food processing operations, such as pumping, mixing, emulsification, and heat transfer. By mastering the principles of fluid mechanics and rheology, chemical engineering professionals and anyone interested in food product design can enhance their understanding of how fluid behavior impacts food quality, processing efficiency, and overall production success.

Whether you are a chemical engineering student, a food processing professional, or simply curious about the science behind food engineering, this subchapter will provide you with a comprehensive overview of fluid mechanics and rheology in food processing. Through real-world examples and practical insights, you will gain the knowledge and skills necessary to navigate the complexities of fluid behavior and optimize food processing operations for superior product design and innovation.

Chapter 3: Food Product Development Process

Understanding Consumer Preferences and Market Trends

In today's rapidly changing world, understanding consumer preferences and market trends is crucial for success in the food industry. As a chemical engineer delving into the world of food engineering, it is important to grasp the dynamics of consumer behavior and the ever-evolving market landscape. This subchapter aims to provide you with a comprehensive overview of how to decipher consumer preferences and stay abreast of market trends, enabling you to create innovative and successful food products.

Consumer preferences are at the heart of product design. By understanding what consumers want and need, you can develop food products that cater to their desires and expectations. This section will take you through the process of analyzing consumer preferences, which includes conducting market research, identifying target demographics, and studying consumer behavior. You will learn how to collect and analyze data to gain insights into consumer preferences, allowing you to make informed decisions during the product development process.

Market trends play a significant role in shaping consumer preferences. By staying up-to-date with the latest trends, you can anticipate shifts in consumer demand and adjust your product offerings accordingly. This subchapter will explore various market trends, such as the growing demand for healthier and more sustainable food options, the rise of plant-based diets, and the increasing interest in ethnic and global flavors. Understanding these trends will empower you to create innovative food products that resonate with consumers and meet their evolving needs.

Additionally, this subchapter will delve into the factors that influence consumer preferences and market trends. You will explore the impact of cultural, social, and economic factors on consumer behavior, as well as the role of advertising and branding in shaping consumer perceptions. Understanding these influences will provide you with a holistic perspective on consumer preferences and enable you to design food products that align with market demands.

To succeed in food product design, it is essential to grasp the nuances of consumer preferences and market trends. By understanding what consumers want and staying attuned to the ever-changing market landscape, you can create food products that captivate consumers and drive business growth. This subchapter will equip you with the knowledge and tools to navigate the complex world of consumer preferences and market trends, enabling you to master the art of food product design and excel in the field of food engineering.

Conceptualizing and Ideating Food Products

In today's fast-paced and ever-evolving food industry, the process of conceptualizing and ideating food products is a crucial step towards creating innovative and successful culinary delights. This subchapter aims to provide a comprehensive understanding of this process, catering not only to the general audience but also specifically to those in the field of chemical engineering.

Conceptualizing a food product involves developing a clear vision of the desired end result. This requires extensive research and analysis of current market trends, consumer preferences, and emerging technologies. By understanding the needs and desires of the target audience, food engineers can begin to conceptualize unique and marketable food products.

Ideating, on the other hand, is the creative process of generating ideas and concepts that align with the initial vision. This involves brainstorming sessions, exploring different ingredients, flavors, textures, and techniques. Chemical engineers play a vital role during this stage as they provide expertise in analyzing the chemical composition of ingredients, evaluating their compatibility, and ensuring the feasibility of the proposed food product.

To aid in the conceptualization and ideation process, various tools and techniques can be employed. These include mind mapping, sensory analysis, trend mapping, and prototyping. Through mind mapping, ideas can be visually organized and interconnected, fostering creativity and innovation. Sensory analysis allows food engineers to evaluate the taste, smell, texture, and appearance of potential food products, ensuring they meet consumer expectations. Trend mapping helps identify emerging food trends and enables engineers to design products that align with these preferences. Prototyping involves creating physical or virtual models of the proposed food product, allowing for testing and refinement before finalizing the concept.

Furthermore, collaboration and cross-disciplinary teamwork are essential during the conceptualization and ideation stage. Bringing together professionals from various fields, such as chemical engineering, culinary arts, food science, and marketing, can lead to a more holistic and successful product development process. By combining their expertise and perspectives, innovative and commercially viable food products can be created.

In conclusion, conceptualizing and ideating food products is a multidimensional process that requires meticulous research, creativity, and collaboration. For chemical engineers, this process involves analyzing the chemical aspects of ingredients and ensuring their compatibility in the final product. By mastering these skills, food engineers can contribute to the creation of groundbreaking and marketable food products that meet the ever-evolving demands of consumers.

Formulation and Recipe Development

In the world of food engineering, formulation and recipe development play a crucial role in creating innovative and successful food products. Whether you are a food scientist, a chemical engineer, or simply an enthusiast looking to experiment in your kitchen, understanding the art and science behind formulation and recipe development is essential.

Formulation refers to the process of designing a food product by determining the ingredients and their quantities. It involves careful consideration of factors such as taste, texture, nutritional profile, shelf life, and cost. A well-formulated product strikes a balance between these elements, creating a harmonious and enjoyable eating experience.

Recipe development, on the other hand, involves the practical application of the formulated product. It is the blueprint that guides the production process, detailing the steps and techniques required to bring the formulation to life. The recipe not only ensures consistency in the final product but also serves as a valuable tool for quality control and scaling up production.

For chemical engineers, formulation and recipe development provide an opportunity to apply their knowledge and skills in optimizing processes and improving efficiency. Their expertise in understanding the interactions between ingredients, heat transfer, and mass transfer can help create more sustainable and cost-effective food products. By utilizing advanced techniques like computational modeling and simulation, chemical engineers can fine-tune formulations and recipes to meet specific requirements, such as reducing energy consumption or minimizing waste.

But formulation and recipe development are not limited to professionals alone. Anyone with a passion for food can dive into this fascinating world and create their own culinary masterpieces. With the right knowledge and a spirit of experimentation, you can develop unique flavors, textures, and presentations that reflect your personal style and preferences. Whether it's recreating a classic dish with a twist or inventing an entirely new creation, formulation and recipe development allow you to unleash your creativity in the kitchen.

In this subchapter, we will explore the principles and techniques behind formulation and recipe development. From understanding ingredient functionality to exploring different processing methods, we will provide you with the tools and insights necessary to create your own food products. Through case studies, practical examples, and expert tips, you will gain a deeper understanding of the intricate and exciting world of food engineering.

So, whether you are an aspiring food scientist, a chemical engineer, or simply someone who loves experimenting in the kitchen, join us on this journey into the realm of formulation and recipe development. Let's unlock the secrets behind creating delicious and innovative food products that captivate the senses and tantalize the taste buds.

Prototyping and Testing

In the world of food engineering, the process of prototyping and testing plays a crucial role in the successful development of new food products. This subchapter will delve into the importance of prototyping and testing, and how it relates to the field of chemical engineering.

Prototyping is the process of creating a preliminary version of a product, which allows designers and engineers to visualize and test their ideas before going into full-scale production. In the context of food product design, prototyping involves creating a prototype of a new food product, which can range from a simple recipe to a more complex formulation.

One of the main reasons why prototyping is essential in food engineering is to ensure that the final product meets the desired specifications in terms of taste, texture, appearance, and functionality. By creating prototypes, engineers can identify any potential issues or shortcomings early in the design process, allowing them to make necessary adjustments and improvements.

Chemical engineering plays a significant role in prototyping and testing food products. Chemical engineers have a deep understanding of the physical and chemical properties of food ingredients, which is crucial in formulating recipes and developing new food products. They can apply their knowledge of chemical reactions, heat transfer, and mass transfer to optimize the production process and ensure the quality of the final product.

Testing is another vital step in the food product development process. Once a prototype is created, it needs to undergo rigorous testing to evaluate its performance and characteristics. This includes sensory testing, where trained panels or consumers assess the taste, texture, aroma, and overall acceptability of the product. Chemical engineers can contribute by analyzing the composition of the prototype, conducting microbiological testing, and assessing the stability and shelf-life of the product.

Prototyping and testing are iterative processes, meaning that multiple rounds of prototyping and testing are often required before a final product is ready for commercialization. This allows engineers to refine the product and address any issues that arise during testing.

In conclusion, prototyping and testing are critical steps in the journey of food product design. Chemical engineers play a significant role in this process, utilizing their knowledge of food chemistry and engineering principles to create prototypes and test them for quality, functionality, and consumer acceptability. By embracing prototyping and testing, food engineers can ensure that their products meet the highest standards and provide consumers with safe, nutritious, and enjoyable food experiences.

Chapter 4: Food Processing Techniques

Thermal Processing: Pasteurization and Sterilization

Thermal processing is a crucial aspect of food engineering that plays a vital role in ensuring the safety and quality of food products. Two commonly used methods of thermal processing are pasteurization and sterilization. In this subchapter, we will delve into the intricacies of these processes and their significance in the field of chemical engineering.

Pasteurization is a thermal processing technique primarily used to eliminate pathogenic microorganisms from food products. It involves heating the food to a specific temperature for a set period, followed by rapid cooling. The objective is to eliminate harmful bacteria, viruses, and parasites without significantly affecting the taste, texture, or nutrient content of the food. Pasteurization is widely used for milk, fruit juices, and other perishable beverages.

Sterilization, on the other hand, is a more intense thermal processing method aimed at completely eradicating all microorganisms, including spore-forming bacteria, yeasts, and molds. It involves subjecting the food to high temperatures for a longer duration than pasteurization. Sterilization is commonly used for canned goods, ready-to-eat meals, and long shelf-life products.

Both pasteurization and sterilization require careful control of time and temperature to achieve the desired microbial reduction while preserving the sensory and nutritional properties of the food. Chemical engineers play a pivotal role in designing and optimizing thermal processing systems. They consider factors such as the heat transfer characteristics of the food, type of microorganisms present, and the desired shelf life to determine the most suitable processing parameters.

Advancements in food engineering have led to the development of novel thermal processing techniques, such as high-pressure processing and pulsed electric field processing. These innovative methods offer alternative ways to pasteurize and sterilize food while minimizing the impact on taste, texture, and nutritional value. Chemical engineers are at the forefront of research and development in this area, continually striving to improve existing processes and develop new ones.

In conclusion, thermal processing techniques like pasteurization and sterilization are essential for ensuring food safety and quality. Chemical engineers play a crucial role in the design and optimization of these processes, considering factors such as heat transfer and microbial reduction. As the field of food engineering continues to evolve, new and innovative thermal processing methods are being developed, paving the way for safer and more nutritious food products for everyone to enjoy.

Non-Thermal Processing: High-Pressure Processing and Pulsed Electric Fields

In the world of food engineering, there are various techniques utilized to process and preserve food products. Among these techniques, non-thermal processing methods have gained significant attention for their ability to extend shelf life and maintain the nutritional quality of food without the use of high temperatures. Two prominent non-thermal processing methods are High-Pressure Processing (HPP) and Pulsed Electric Fields (PEF), which offer unique advantages in food preservation and quality enhancement.

High-Pressure Processing (HPP) involves subjecting food products to high pressure levels, typically between 100 and 1000 MPa, to inactivate microorganisms, enzymes, and other spoilage agents. This process is known for its ability to preserve the sensory attributes and nutritional content of food while ensuring safety. HPP is particularly effective in preserving products like fruit juices, guacamole, and ready-to-eat meats, as it eliminates the need for high-temperature pasteurization, thereby preventing the degradation of flavors, vitamins, and other heat-sensitive compounds. HPP also offers an extended shelf life, allowing manufacturers to meet consumer demands for minimally processed, yet safe food products.

Pulsed Electric Fields (PEF) is another non-thermal processing technique that involves applying short, intense electric pulses to food products. These pulses disrupt the cell membranes of microorganisms, leading to their inactivation while maintaining the sensory and nutritional qualities of the food. PEF has shown great potential in the preservation of liquid and semi-solid foods, such as milk, fruit purees, and soups. By reducing the microbial load and inactivating spoilage enzymes, PEF extends the shelf life of these products while preserving their original taste, color, and texture.

Both HPP and PEF techniques offer significant advantages over traditional thermal processing methods. By using pressure or electric fields instead of heat, these methods minimize the loss of nutrients, flavors, and textures that occur during thermal treatments. Moreover, non-thermal processing methods are considered more environmentally friendly, as they use less energy and reduce greenhouse gas emissions compared to thermal techniques.

For chemical engineering professionals and enthusiasts, understanding non-thermal processing methods like HPP and PEF is crucial in designing and optimizing food production processes. These techniques present opportunities to develop innovative and sustainable food products that meet consumer demands for both safety and quality. By harnessing the power of pressure and electric fields, chemical engineers can contribute to the advancement of food processing technology and drive the future of the food industry towards healthier, more sustainable practices.

Drying and Dehydration Techniques

In the world of food engineering, drying and dehydration techniques play a crucial role in the preservation and enhancement of various food products. These techniques are employed to remove moisture from food items, thereby extending their shelf life, improving their texture, enhancing their flavor, and increasing their portability. From fruits and vegetables to meats and grains, drying and dehydration techniques are utilized across a wide range of food categories.

One of the most common methods of drying is air drying. This technique involves exposing food products to ambient air, allowing the moisture to naturally evaporate. Air drying is a cost-effective and energy-efficient method, making it widely used in both industrial and domestic settings. However, air drying can be time-consuming, and its effectiveness depends on factors such as temperature, humidity, and airflow.

Another popular technique is freeze drying, also known as lyophilization. This process involves freezing the food product and then subjecting it to a vacuum environment, where the frozen water content is directly converted into vapor without passing through the liquid phase. Freeze drying helps retain the food's nutritional value, flavor, and texture, making it ideal for delicate items like fruits, vegetables, and herbs. However, freeze drying is a complex and expensive process, primarily used in industrial settings.

Spray drying is a technique commonly used for the production of powders. In this method, a liquid food concentrate is atomized into tiny droplets, which are then rapidly dried by hot air. The moisture evaporates, leaving behind a dry powder that can be easily stored and reconstituted with water. Spray drying is extensively used in the production of milk powders, coffee, and instant soups.

Chemical engineers play a vital role in developing and optimizing these drying and dehydration techniques. They work on improving efficiency, reducing energy consumption, and enhancing the overall quality of dried food products. By understanding the principles of heat transfer, mass transfer, and fluid dynamics, chemical engineers can design and optimize drying processes tailored to specific food items.

In conclusion, drying and dehydration techniques are essential in the world of food engineering. They enable the preservation, enhancement, and portability of various food products. Whether it is air drying, freeze drying, or spray drying, these methods provide solutions for extending shelf life, improving texture, and enhancing flavors. Chemical engineers continue to play a significant role in advancing these techniques, making them more efficient and sustainable for the food industry as a whole.

Fermentation and Bioprocessing

In the ever-evolving world of food engineering, one of the most fascinating and widely used techniques is fermentation and bioprocessing. This subchapter aims to introduce the concept of fermentation and its applications in the food industry. Whether you are a student of chemical engineering or simply someone intrigued by the science behind food production, this subchapter will provide you with a comprehensive understanding of this essential process.

Fermentation is a natural metabolic process that converts carbohydrates into various products, such as alcohol, organic acids, or gases, using microorganisms like bacteria or yeast. This process has been used for centuries in the production of staple food items such as bread, cheese, and beer. However, in recent years, fermentation has gained significant attention in the realm of food product design due to its ability to enhance flavors, improve nutritional values, and extend shelf life.

This subchapter will explore the various types of fermentation, including alcoholic fermentation, lactic acid fermentation, and acetic acid fermentation, among others. We will delve into the factors influencing fermentation, such as temperature, pH, and oxygen availability, and how these factors can be manipulated to achieve desired outcomes. Additionally, we will discuss the important role of microorganisms in fermentation and how different strains can be selected for specific product characteristics.

Furthermore, bioprocessing, a subfield of fermentation, will be explored in detail. Bioprocessing involves using biological systems, such as enzymes or microorganisms, to produce or modify food products. This section will discuss the different techniques involved in bioprocessing, such as immobilization, genetic engineering, and downstream processing. We will also touch on the potential challenges and ethical considerations associated with bioprocessing.

Throughout this subchapter, real-world examples and case studies will be provided to illustrate the practical applications of fermentation and bioprocessing in food engineering. From the production of probiotics to the development of plant-based meat alternatives, these examples will showcase the versatility and innovation that fermentation brings to the table.

Whether you are a chemical engineering student or simply curious about the science behind your favorite food products, this subchapter will serve as a valuable resource. By delving into the world of fermentation and bioprocessing, you will gain a deeper understanding of the techniques and processes that shape the food industry, and hopefully, inspire you to explore new frontiers in food product design.

Chapter 5: Food Packaging and Preservation

Packaging Materials and Technologies

In the world of food engineering, the role of packaging materials and technologies cannot be overstated. Packaging serves as the first point of contact between consumers and food products, influencing their perception and overall experience. This subchapter aims to provide an overview of the various packaging materials and technologies used in the food industry, catering to a wide audience, including those interested in chemical engineering.

Packaging materials play a critical role in preserving the quality and safety of food products. They act as a barrier against external factors such as moisture, oxygen, light, and microorganisms, preventing spoilage and extending shelf life. One of the commonly used packaging materials is plastic, which offers excellent flexibility, durability, and cost-effectiveness. However, concerns about its environmental impact have led to the development of alternative materials such as biodegradable plastics, paper-based materials, and innovative bio-based polymers.

Another important aspect of packaging is its functionality. Packaging technologies have evolved to meet the demands of modern consumers, who seek convenience and ease of use. Advanced packaging technologies include modified atmosphere packaging (MAP), which alters the composition of gases within the package to slow down the growth of spoilage-causing microorganisms. This technique is particularly useful for extending the shelf life of fresh produce and processed foods.

Furthermore, active packaging technologies have gained popularity in recent years. These technologies incorporate active substances into packaging materials, providing additional benefits such as antimicrobial properties, oxygen scavenging, and moisture control. These active packaging solutions not only enhance food safety but also improve product quality and extend shelf life.

The subchapter will also delve into the latest trends and innovations in packaging materials and technologies. This includes smart packaging, which integrates sensors and intelligent systems to monitor the quality and condition of food products throughout the supply chain. Additionally, sustainable packaging solutions that focus on reducing waste and environmental impact will be explored.

By understanding the intricacies of packaging materials and technologies, both food engineers and chemical engineering enthusiasts can contribute to the development of innovative and sustainable packaging solutions. This subchapter aims to equip readers with the knowledge necessary to navigate the dynamic world of food packaging, ultimately enhancing the overall consumer experience and ensuring the safety and quality of food products.

Shelf-Life Extension Techniques

In the world of food engineering, shelf-life extension techniques are of utmost importance to ensure the safety and quality of food products. These techniques play a crucial role in preserving the taste, texture, and nutritional value of various food items, ultimately contributing to the overall satisfaction of consumers. In this subchapter, we will delve into the different methods employed to extend the shelf life of food products, exploring the realm of chemical engineering in the food industry.

One of the most widely used techniques in shelf-life extension is the application of food preservatives. Chemical engineers are at the forefront of developing and implementing safe and effective preservatives that inhibit the growth of bacteria, molds, and yeasts, thereby preventing spoilage. These preservatives can be natural or synthetic, and their selection depends on the specific food product and desired shelf life. By understanding the interactions between preservatives and food matrices, chemical engineers can optimize formulations to maintain the quality and safety of food products.

Another essential technique employed in shelf-life extension is packaging technology. Chemical engineers work closely with packaging experts to develop innovative packaging materials that improve product shelf life. Oxygen scavengers, moisture barriers, and antimicrobial films are just a few examples of packaging solutions designed to protect food products from deterioration. These materials are carefully engineered to create a controlled environment, preventing the entry of harmful microorganisms and delaying oxidation processes.

Furthermore, chemical engineers play a pivotal role in developing and optimizing food processing technologies. Techniques such as pasteurization, sterilization, and high-pressure processing are employed to eliminate or reduce the microbial load in food products, thereby increasing their shelf life. By meticulously studying the kinetics of microbial inactivation and understanding the underlying chemical reactions, engineers can determine the optimal parameters for processing, ensuring both safety and quality.

In this subchapter, we will explore the various techniques utilized by chemical engineers to extend the shelf life of food products. Understanding the principles behind these techniques not only helps professionals in the field but also provides valuable knowledge for consumers. By grasping the importance of shelf-life extension techniques, individuals can make informed decisions about the safety and quality of the food they consume.

Whether you are a chemical engineering student, a professional in the food industry, or simply an individual interested in the science behind food preservation, this subchapter will provide you with a comprehensive overview of shelf-life extension techniques. Join us on this journey into the world of food engineering, where chemical innovations contribute to the longevity and deliciousness of our favorite food products.

Packaging Design and Consumer Appeal

In the competitive world of food engineering, packaging design plays a crucial role in capturing consumer attention and influencing purchasing decisions. The way a product is presented can greatly impact its success in the market, making it imperative for food engineers to understand the significance of packaging design and its correlation with consumer appeal.

Packaging design encompasses various elements such as visual aesthetics, functionality, and sustainability. When it comes to food products, the packaging should not only be visually appealing but also provide convenience and protection to the contents within. A well-designed package should effectively communicate the brand's message and create a memorable impression on consumers.

Visual aesthetics play a vital role in attracting consumers. Colors, graphics, and typography can convey the product's qualities and create an emotional connection with the target audience. For instance, vibrant colors and playful designs may appeal to children, while elegant and sophisticated packaging may attract adults. Packaging should also reflect the product's quality and freshness, as consumers often associate these attributes with visually appealing packaging.

Functionality is another crucial aspect of packaging design. Consumers seek convenience, ease of use, and resealability in food packaging. A well-designed package should be user-friendly, allowing easy access to the product and providing clear instructions for usage. Additionally, packaging should ensure the preservation of taste, aroma, and nutritional value of the food product, enhancing the overall consumer experience.

Sustainability is an emerging trend in packaging design, driven by consumer demand for eco-friendly solutions. Food engineers must consider the environmental impact of packaging materials and strive to develop innovative, sustainable alternatives. Biodegradable, compostable, and recyclable materials are gaining popularity, as they align with consumers' growing concerns about the environment. Incorporating sustainable packaging solutions not only appeals to environmentally conscious consumers but also contributes to a brand's reputation and corporate social responsibility.

In conclusion, packaging design is an essential aspect of food product development, influencing consumer appeal and purchase decisions. Food engineers must focus on creating visually appealing, functional, and sustainable packaging solutions that resonate with their target audience. By mastering the art of packaging design, food engineers can enhance the success of their products in a competitive market, ultimately contributing to the growth and advancement of the field of food engineering.

Chapter 6: Food Quality and Safety

Quality Parameters and Assessment Methods

In the fascinating world of food engineering, ensuring the quality and safety of food products is of paramount importance. This subchapter delves into the fundamental aspects of quality parameters and assessment methods, providing a comprehensive understanding of how chemical engineering principles are applied to guarantee the highest standards in food product design.

Quality parameters serve as benchmarks for evaluating the characteristics and attributes of food products. These parameters encompass various factors such as taste, texture, appearance, nutritional value, shelf life, and safety. Through an in-depth analysis of these parameters, food engineers can optimize the design and production processes to create products that meet the expectations and preferences of consumers.

Assessment methods play a crucial role in quantifying and evaluating the quality parameters of food products. Chemical engineering techniques enable the precise measurement and analysis of these parameters, ensuring that the final product meets the desired specifications. Techniques such as sensory analysis, chemical analysis, microbiological analysis, and physical testing are employed to assess the taste, composition, microbial load, and physical properties of food products.

Sensory analysis involves trained panelists who evaluate the taste, aroma, texture, and appearance of food products through sensory perception. This method provides valuable insights into consumer preferences and helps optimize the sensory attributes of the final product.

Chemical analysis involves the measurement and analysis of the chemical composition of food products, including the levels of nutrients, additives, contaminants, and flavor compounds. This method ensures that the nutritional value and safety of food products are in compliance with regulatory standards.

Microbiological analysis focuses on assessing the microbial load and the presence of pathogens in food products. By employing various testing methods, food engineers can ensure that the final product is free from harmful microorganisms, reducing the risk of foodborne illnesses.

Physical testing involves measuring the physical properties of food products, such as viscosity, rheology, hardness, and color. These properties are crucial in determining the texture, appearance, and overall sensory experience of the product.

With a clear understanding of quality parameters and assessment methods, food engineers can design and develop food products that not only meet regulatory requirements but also exceed consumer expectations. By continuously evaluating and optimizing these parameters, they can create innovative and safe food products that cater to diverse consumer needs.

Whether you are a student of chemical engineering, a professional in the field, or simply an enthusiastic food lover, this subchapter provides valuable insights into the fascinating world of food engineering and the critical role played by quality parameters and assessment methods in ensuring the highest standards of food product design.

Food Safety Regulations and Compliance

In today's globalized world, ensuring the safety of our food is of paramount importance. Food safety regulations and compliance play a crucial role in safeguarding public health and maintaining the trust of consumers. This subchapter explores the intricate web of regulations and the importance of compliance in the field of food engineering.

Food safety regulations are designed to prevent foodborne illnesses, protect consumers from potential hazards, and promote the production of safe and wholesome food products. These regulations are drafted by government agencies and regulatory bodies, such as the Food and Drug Administration (FDA) in the United States, the European Food Safety Authority (EFSA), and the World Health Organization (WHO). They establish guidelines and standards for various aspects of food production, including manufacturing processes, packaging, labeling, and storage.

Compliance with these regulations is not only a legal requirement but also a moral obligation for food engineers and manufacturers. By adhering to these standards, they demonstrate their commitment to producing high-quality, safe, and nutritious food products. Compliance involves implementing robust quality control systems, conducting regular inspections, and maintaining detailed records of all aspects of food production.

Chemical engineering plays a vital role in ensuring compliance with food safety regulations. It involves the application of scientific principles and engineering techniques to design and optimize food manufacturing processes. Chemical engineers work closely with food scientists to develop innovative techniques that minimize the risk of contamination and ensure the safety and quality of food products.

One of the key challenges in compliance is the constantly evolving nature of regulations. As scientific knowledge advances and new risks emerge, regulations are updated to address these concerns. Food engineers must stay up-to-date with the latest regulations and adapt their processes accordingly. This requires continuous learning, training, and investment in research and development to ensure compliance.

In conclusion, food safety regulations and compliance are vital for protecting public health and maintaining consumer confidence. Chemical engineers play a crucial role in ensuring compliance by applying their expertise to develop safe and efficient food manufacturing processes. By adhering to these regulations, food engineers contribute to the production of safe and wholesome food products that benefit everyone.

Food Traceability and Supply Chain Management

In today's globalized world, the food industry faces numerous challenges in ensuring the safety, quality, and authenticity of products. One of the critical aspects of achieving this goal is through effective food traceability and supply chain management. This subchapter delves into the intricacies of these processes, highlighting their importance in the field of chemical engineering.

Food traceability refers to the ability to track and trace the movement of food products along the supply chain. It involves capturing and recording data at various stages, including production, processing, distribution, and retail. This data provides vital information about the origin, ingredients, processing methods, and distribution channels of food products. By implementing a robust traceability system, chemical engineers can identify and address potential risks, such as contamination, counterfeiting, or adulteration, thus safeguarding consumer health and brand reputation.

Supply chain management, on the other hand, encompasses the coordination and optimization of all activities involved in the production and delivery of food products. It involves managing the flow of goods, information, and finances from the sourcing of raw materials to the final consumption. Chemical engineers play a significant role in ensuring the efficiency, sustainability, and cost-effectiveness of the supply chain. They employ innovative techniques, such as process optimization, logistics planning, and waste reduction strategies, to enhance the overall performance of the food industry.

The integration of food traceability and supply chain management is crucial for chemical engineers to address the challenges posed by globalization, complex supply networks, and stringent regulatory requirements. By implementing advanced technologies, such as blockchain, Internet of Things (IoT), and artificial intelligence (AI), chemical engineers can create a transparent and secure traceability system that ensures the integrity of food products. These technologies enable real-time data collection, analysis, and sharing, facilitating quick response and decision-making in case of emergencies or recalls.

Furthermore, effective supply chain management allows chemical engineers to optimize processes, reduce waste, and minimize environmental impacts. By adopting sustainable practices, such as energy-efficient transportation, waste reduction, and recycling, they can contribute to a more sustainable and resilient food system. Additionally, supply chain management strategies, such as just-in-time delivery and inventory management, help minimize costs, improve resource allocation, and enhance customer satisfaction.

In conclusion, food traceability and supply chain management are indispensable aspects of the food industry, and chemical engineers play a vital role in driving their implementation. By leveraging advanced technologies and adopting sustainable practices, chemical engineers can ensure the safety, quality, and integrity of food products while optimizing the efficiency and sustainability of the supply chain. This subchapter provides a comprehensive overview of these processes, equipping chemical engineering professionals with the knowledge and tools necessary to master the complexities of food product design.

Chapter 7: Sensory Evaluation and Consumer Testing

Sensory Perception and Evaluation Techniques

In the fascinating field of food engineering, one of the most crucial aspects is understanding and optimizing the sensory perception of food products. This subchapter delves into the world of sensory perception and evaluation techniques, shedding light on the intricate relationship between chemical engineering and the human senses.

The sensory perception of food plays a pivotal role in determining its overall quality, consumer acceptance, and market success. It encompasses the evaluation of taste, texture, aroma, appearance, and even sound. As chemical engineers, it is imperative to comprehend the underlying mechanisms that influence sensory perception to develop innovative and desirable food products.

To achieve this, a range of evaluation techniques are employed. One such technique is sensory analysis, which involves a group of trained panelists who assess and quantify the sensory attributes of food products through rigorous testing. These panelists are equipped with a refined palate and a deep understanding of the parameters that affect taste, texture, aroma, and appearance. By utilizing statistical methods, sensory evaluation results can be objectively interpreted and utilized to optimize food product design and formulation.

Additionally, instrumental techniques play a significant role in evaluating sensory attributes. These techniques employ advanced technology to measure and analyze specific sensory parameters, such as texture analyzers to assess mouthfeel or gas chromatography to analyze aroma compounds. By integrating these instrumental techniques with chemical engineering principles, a comprehensive understanding of the sensory perception of food products can be achieved.

Understanding the sensory perception of food products also involves exploring the psychological and physiological aspects of human perception. Factors such as cultural background, individual preferences, and physiological differences influence how individuals perceive taste, aroma, and texture. By considering these factors during food product design, chemical engineers can create products that cater to a diverse range of consumers.

In conclusion, sensory perception and evaluation techniques are indispensable tools for chemical engineers in the world of food product design. By comprehending the intricacies of sensory perception, engineers can optimize the taste, texture, aroma, and appearance of food products, ensuring their success in the market. Through the integration of sensory analysis, instrumental techniques, and an understanding of psychological and physiological factors, chemical engineers can embark on a journey toward mastering the art of food product design.

Consumer Testing and Market Research

In the ever-evolving world of food engineering, understanding the needs and preferences of consumers is paramount to the success of any food product. Consumer testing and market research play a crucial role in this process, helping food engineers and chemical professionals design and develop products that truly resonate with their target audience.

Consumer testing involves gathering feedback from potential consumers through various methods, such as surveys, focus groups, and taste testing. This invaluable feedback allows engineers to gauge consumer preferences, identify areas for improvement, and make informed decisions in the product development process.

One of the primary goals of consumer testing is to ensure that the final product meets the expectations and demands of the target market. By gathering feedback early on, engineers can identify potential issues or areas of improvement before the product hits the shelves. This not only helps in reducing the risk of failure but also saves valuable time and resources.

Market research, on the other hand, focuses on analyzing the broader market landscape to identify trends, consumer behavior, and potential opportunities. Chemical engineers can utilize market research to understand the competitive landscape, identify gaps in the market, and make strategic decisions regarding product positioning and marketing strategies.

By combining consumer testing and market research, food engineers can gain comprehensive insights into consumer preferences, needs, and desires. This knowledge enables them to create products that not only meet consumer expectations but also stand out in the highly competitive food industry.

Moreover, consumer testing and market research also play a crucial role in ensuring the safety and quality of food products. By gathering feedback and conducting sensory evaluations, engineers can identify potential issues related to taste, texture, or appearance that may affect consumer perception. This allows them to refine the formulation and optimize the production process to deliver safe, high-quality products to consumers.

In conclusion, consumer testing and market research are essential tools in the field of food engineering. By understanding the needs, preferences, and behavior of consumers, chemical engineers can design and develop innovative products that cater to the demands of the market. Additionally, these practices help ensure the safety and quality of food products, ultimately leading to the success of food engineering endeavors.

Incorporating Feedback into Food Product Design

Welcome to the subchapter on "Incorporating Feedback into Food Product Design" from the book "Mastering Food Product Design: A Journey into the World of Food Engineering." This subchapter is specifically tailored to the audience of "everyone," with a particular focus on the niche of Chemical Engineering.

Designing food products that cater to the ever-evolving tastes and preferences of consumers is a challenging task. In this subchapter, we will explore the importance of incorporating feedback into the food product design process and how Chemical Engineering can play a significant role in achieving this goal.

Feedback from consumers is crucial in understanding their needs, desires, and expectations. By actively seeking and incorporating feedback, food product designers can create products that resonate with their target audience. To begin with, conducting surveys, focus groups, and taste tests can provide valuable insights into consumer preferences. This information can then be used to guide the formulation and development of food products.

Chemical Engineering is a fundamental discipline that contributes to the design and optimization of food products. It encompasses various aspects such as ingredient selection, processing techniques, and product stability. By incorporating feedback into the food product design process, Chemical Engineers can enhance the sensory attributes, nutritional value, and overall quality of the final product.

One of the key aspects of incorporating feedback is sensory evaluation. Chemical Engineers can collaborate with sensory scientists to conduct sensory panels and evaluate the sensory properties of food products.

By understanding the sensory preferences of consumers, designers can make informed decisions about flavor profiles, texture, color, and other sensory attributes.

Furthermore, Chemical Engineering techniques such as product testing and quality control can help ensure that the designed food products meet the desired specifications. This can be achieved through rigorous testing, analysis, and optimization of the manufacturing processes. By continuously monitoring and improving the quality of food products based on consumer feedback, Chemical Engineers can contribute to the development of successful and marketable products.

In conclusion, incorporating feedback into food product design is essential for creating products that resonate with consumers. Chemical Engineering plays a vital role in this process by providing the technical expertise required to optimize the sensory attributes, nutritional value, and overall quality of food products. By actively seeking and incorporating feedback, Chemical Engineers can contribute to the development of innovative and consumer-driven food products.

Remember, the success of a food product lies in its ability to satisfy the ever-evolving tastes and preferences of consumers. So, let us embrace feedback and work together to create food products that not only meet but exceed consumer expectations.

Chapter 8: Novel Food Product Design

Functional Foods and Nutraceuticals

In recent years, there has been a growing interest in functional foods and nutraceuticals among consumers worldwide. These specialized food products have gained popularity due to their potential health benefits beyond basic nutrition. This subchapter will explore the concept of functional foods and nutraceuticals, their significance in the food industry, and their relevance to the field of chemical engineering.

Functional foods are defined as foods that provide additional health benefits beyond their basic nutritional value. These foods often contain bioactive compounds, such as vitamins, minerals, dietary fibers, or antioxidants, which are known to have positive effects on human health. Nutraceuticals, on the other hand, refer to products derived from food sources that provide health benefits when consumed in specific quantities. These may include dietary supplements, fortified foods, or medicinal foods.

The significance of functional foods and nutraceuticals lies in their potential to prevent or manage chronic diseases, improve overall well-being, and enhance the quality of life. For instance, certain functional foods have been found to reduce the risk of heart disease, lower blood pressure, boost immune function, or improve cognitive function. These health benefits have led to increased consumer demand for such products, creating a niche market in the food industry.

Chemical engineering plays a crucial role in the development and production of functional foods and nutraceuticals. From the formulation of novel food products to the extraction and purification of bioactive compounds, chemical engineers contribute their expertise in various stages of the manufacturing process. They utilize their knowledge of chemistry, biology, and process engineering to optimize the nutritional content, stability, and sensory properties of these specialized food items.

Furthermore, chemical engineers are involved in the development of innovative techniques for the delivery and encapsulation of bioactive compounds, ensuring their bioavailability and efficacy in the human body. They also play a vital role in the safety assessment and regulatory compliance of functional foods and nutraceuticals, ensuring that these products meet the required standards and do not pose any health risks to consumers.

In conclusion, functional foods and nutraceuticals have emerged as a significant trend in the food industry, catering to the increasing consumer demand for health-promoting food products. Chemical engineering plays a crucial role in the development, production, and quality assurance of these specialized food items. As the field of functional foods continues to evolve, chemical engineers will continue to contribute their expertise to meet the growing needs and expectations of consumers seeking to enhance their health and well-being through their dietary choices.

Plant-Based and Alternative Protein Products

The world of food engineering has witnessed a significant shift in recent years, with increasing interest and demand for plant-based and alternative protein products. This subchapter aims to explore this emerging trend, delving into the various aspects of plant-based proteins and their potential impact on the food industry. Whether you are a food enthusiast, a chemical engineer, or simply curious about the future of food, this subchapter will provide you with valuable insights into this exciting field.

Plant-based protein products are gaining popularity due to several reasons. Firstly, they offer a sustainable alternative to traditional animal-based protein sources, reducing the environmental impact associated with livestock production. Additionally, plant-based proteins are often cholesterol-free and lower in saturated fats, making them a healthier option for individuals concerned about their dietary choices.

One of the key challenges in developing plant-based protein products lies in achieving the desired taste and texture, as they differ significantly from animal-based proteins. Chemical engineers play a crucial role in this process, employing their expertise to design innovative methods and technologies for extracting, isolating, and modifying plant proteins. By understanding the molecular properties of plant proteins, engineers can optimize their functionalities, improving their sensory attributes and making them more appealing to a broader consumer base.

Moreover, this subchapter discusses the utilization of alternative protein sources, such as algae, fungi, and insects, as potential solutions to the growing demand for protein. These unconventional sources offer unique nutritional profiles and can be cultivated with minimal environmental impact. Chemical engineers, with their knowledge of bioconversion and bioprocessing, are at the forefront of developing sustainable methods for utilizing these alternative protein sources and transforming them into viable food products.

Furthermore, the subchapter explores the formulation and processing techniques employed in the production of plant-based protein products. From extrusion and high-pressure processing to fermentation and enzymatic hydrolysis, chemical engineers are continually innovating to create products that mimic the taste, texture, and functionality of animal-based proteins. Additionally, they address challenges related to stability, shelf-life, and sensory attributes to ensure that consumers have access to high-quality plant-based protein products.

In conclusion, plant-based and alternative protein products are revolutionizing the food industry, offering sustainable, nutritious, and delicious alternatives to traditional animal-based proteins. Chemical engineers play a pivotal role in this journey, applying their expertise to extract, modify, and process plant proteins and explore unconventional protein sources. Whether you are a food enthusiast or a chemical engineer, this subchapter provides valuable insights into the exciting world of plant-based and alternative protein products, highlighting the immense potential for innovation and change in the way we produce and consume food.

Sustainable and Eco-Friendly Food Innovations

In recent years, there has been a growing concern about the impact of our food systems on the environment. As the global population continues to increase, it is becoming increasingly important to find sustainable and eco-friendly solutions to feed the world. This subchapter explores the various innovative approaches in food engineering that address this pressing issue.

One of the key areas of focus in sustainable food innovation is reducing food waste. According to the Food and Agriculture Organization (FAO) of the United Nations, approximately one-third of all food produced for human consumption is wasted. This not only puts a strain on our resources but also contributes to greenhouse gas emissions. Food engineers are now developing technologies and processes to minimize waste throughout the food supply chain, from production to consumption. These include improved packaging techniques, efficient storage systems, and smart food tracking systems.

Another significant aspect of sustainable food innovation is finding alternative sources of protein. Animal agriculture is a major contributor to greenhouse gas emissions and deforestation. Food engineers are exploring plant-based proteins, such as soy, lentils, and quinoa, as well as developing techniques to produce protein from alternative sources like algae and insects. These innovations not only reduce the environmental impact of food production but also offer healthier and more sustainable dietary choices.

Furthermore, sustainable food innovation involves employing energy-efficient processes in food manufacturing. Chemical engineers play a crucial role in optimizing processes to reduce energy consumption and greenhouse gas emissions. They utilize advanced technologies, such as heat recovery systems, renewable energy sources, and intelligent automation, to make food production more energy-efficient and environmentally friendly.

Additionally, sustainable packaging solutions are being developed to minimize the use of single-use plastics and other non-recyclable materials. Food engineers are exploring biodegradable and compostable packaging materials made from renewable resources, such as plant-based polymers and cellulose fibers. These innovations help reduce the environmental impact of packaging waste and contribute to a more circular economy.

In conclusion, sustainable and eco-friendly food innovations are crucial in addressing the challenges posed by our current food systems. Through reducing food waste, finding alternative protein sources, optimizing energy consumption, and developing sustainable packaging solutions, food engineers are playing a vital role in creating a more sustainable and environmentally friendly future. By embracing these innovations, we can ensure that future generations have access to nutritious food while minimizing our impact on the planet.

Chapter 9: Scaling up and Commercialization

Pilot Plant Operations and Scale-Up Considerations

Introduction:

In the world of food engineering, the development of new food products is a crucial process that requires careful planning and execution. One essential step in this process is pilot plant operations and scale-up considerations. This subchapter will delve into the intricacies of pilot plant operations and provide insights into the key considerations for successful scale-up in the field of food engineering.

Understanding Pilot Plant Operations:

Pilot plant operations serve as a bridge between the laboratory-scale experiments and full-scale industrial production. It allows food engineers to test and refine their product designs in a controlled environment before investing in large-scale production facilities. In this phase, various parameters such as process efficiency, product quality, and safety can be assessed and optimized.

Key Considerations for Scale-Up:

1. Process Validation: Before scaling up, it is crucial to validate the manufacturing process. This involves conducting extensive tests to ensure that the product can be consistently produced at the desired quality, safety, and efficiency levels. This validation process helps identify any potential bottlenecks or challenges that may arise during full-scale production.

2. Equipment Selection: Choosing the right equipment for scale-up is vital. Factors such as production capacity, efficiency, and compatibility with the product's characteristics must be considered. Proper

equipment selection ensures that the process can be replicated on a larger scale without compromising product quality.

3. Ingredient Sourcing: Scaling up production often requires sourcing ingredients in larger quantities. It is essential to establish relationships with reliable suppliers to ensure consistent quality and availability. Additionally, any changes in ingredient sourcing must be carefully evaluated to maintain the desired product attributes.

4. Process Optimization: Scaling up a process often involves modifications to maximize efficiency and productivity. It is crucial to optimize critical process parameters while maintaining product quality. This may involve adjusting temperature, pressure, mixing times, or other variables to achieve the desired results.

5. Quality Control: Implementing a robust quality control system is essential during scale-up. Regular testing and analysis should be performed to ensure that the product meets the established specifications. Quality control measures help identify any deviations and enable corrective actions to be taken promptly.

Conclusion:

Pilot plant operations and scale-up considerations are essential for successful food product design. By carefully addressing these considerations, food engineers can ensure that their products meet the desired quality, safety, and efficiency standards when transitioning from lab-scale to large-scale production. With a thorough understanding of these processes, chemical engineering professionals and other interested readers can gain valuable insights into the complexities of food engineering and master the art of designing innovative food products.

Cost Analysis and Economic Feasibility

In the world of food engineering, understanding the cost analysis and economic feasibility of a food product is crucial for success. This subchapter will delve into the various factors that need to be considered when conducting a cost analysis and determining the economic feasibility of a food product.

Cost analysis is the process of evaluating the expenses associated with the production, distribution, and marketing of a food product. It involves assessing both the direct and indirect costs involved in bringing a product to the market. Direct costs include raw materials, packaging, labor, and equipment, while indirect costs encompass overhead expenses such as utilities, rent, and administrative costs. By breaking down these costs, food engineers can gain a comprehensive understanding of the financial implications of their product.

Economic feasibility refers to the assessment of whether a food product is financially viable. It involves analyzing the potential profitability of the product by comparing the projected revenue to the estimated costs. This analysis takes into account market demand, competition, pricing strategies, and potential barriers to entry. Food engineers need to determine if the product can generate sufficient revenue to cover its costs and provide a reasonable return on investment.

When conducting a cost analysis and economic feasibility study, food engineers must consider various aspects. They should analyze the market demand for the product and assess its potential growth and profitability. Understanding consumer preferences, trends, and competitor offerings is crucial in determining the product's market potential.

Additionally, engineers must evaluate the production process and identify potential cost-saving measures. This may involve optimizing the use of raw materials, reducing waste, streamlining production operations, or implementing automation technologies. By identifying areas for cost reduction, engineers can enhance the economic feasibility of the product.

Moreover, food engineers must consider the impact of external factors such as government regulations, taxes, and subsidies. These factors can significantly influence the cost structure and profitability of a food product. Understanding and adapting to these external forces is essential in ensuring the long-term economic viability of the product.

In conclusion, cost analysis and economic feasibility are vital components of food product design. By carefully evaluating the costs associated with production and assessing the product's market potential, food engineers can determine the viability and profitability of their creations. This subchapter provides an in-depth exploration of the factors to consider when conducting a cost analysis and economic feasibility study. It is an essential resource for anyone interested in mastering the art of food product design, particularly those in the field of chemical engineering.

Manufacturing Process Optimization

In today's fast-paced and competitive food industry, it is crucial for manufacturers to constantly strive for efficiency and productivity. This is where manufacturing process optimization plays a vital role. By streamlining and fine-tuning various aspects of the production process, manufacturers can not only enhance product quality but also reduce costs and maximize profitability.

The manufacturing process optimization techniques discussed in this subchapter will be of immense value to individuals from all walks of life, regardless of their background or expertise. Whether you are a seasoned professional in the food industry or a student studying chemical engineering, this chapter will provide you with valuable insights and practical tips to optimize the manufacturing process.

For chemical engineering professionals, understanding the intricacies of food engineering is essential, as it allows them to apply their knowledge and skills to the unique challenges and requirements of the food industry. This subchapter will delve into various aspects of manufacturing process optimization, such as improving production efficiency, reducing waste, and ensuring product consistency and safety.

Furthermore, this chapter will explore the use of advanced technologies and tools that can be employed to optimize the manufacturing process. From automation and robotics to data analytics and artificial intelligence, these cutting-edge solutions have the potential to revolutionize the way food products are manufactured.

Moreover, this subchapter will discuss the importance of collaboration and cross-functional teamwork in achieving manufacturing process optimization. With inputs from different departments and stakeholders, manufacturers can identify bottlenecks, implement innovative solutions, and drive continuous improvement throughout the production process.

By embracing the principles of manufacturing process optimization, manufacturers can unlock significant benefits. These include higher production yields, improved product quality, reduced energy consumption, and enhanced sustainability. Moreover, by optimizing the manufacturing process, manufacturers can meet the ever-increasing consumer demands for safe, high-quality, and sustainable food products.

In conclusion, this subchapter serves as a comprehensive guide for individuals interested in mastering the art of food product design and manufacturing process optimization. Whether you are a chemical engineering professional or simply someone who wants to gain a deeper understanding of the food industry, this chapter will equip you with the knowledge and tools needed to excel in this dynamic field.

Chapter 10: Future Trends in Food Engineering

Emerging Technologies and Innovations

In today's rapidly advancing world, technological advancements are revolutionizing every aspect of our lives, including the field of food engineering. From the farm to the table, innovative technologies are enhancing the way we produce, process, and consume food. This subchapter explores the fascinating world of emerging technologies and innovations that are shaping the future of the food industry.

One of the most exciting areas of innovation in food engineering is the development of sustainable and efficient farming practices. With the global population expected to reach 9 billion by 2050, traditional farming methods will not be able to meet the demands for food. As a result, technologies such as vertical farming, hydroponics, and aquaponics are gaining momentum. These methods allow for the cultivation of crops in controlled environments, using minimal land, water, and resources. By leveraging technology, farmers can produce higher yields, reduce waste, and ensure year-round crop availability.

In the processing and manufacturing sector, emerging technologies are transforming how we transform raw ingredients into finished food products. One such innovation is high-pressure processing (HPP), which uses extreme pressure to kill bacteria and extend the shelf life of products while preserving their nutritional value. HPP eliminates the need for heat or chemical additives, making it an ideal method for producing healthy and natural foods. Furthermore, advancements in nanotechnology are enabling the creation of novel food structures and textures, enhancing both the sensory experience and nutritional content of products.

The rise of the Internet of Things (IoT) has also had a significant impact on the food industry. Smart sensors and connected devices are being used to monitor and optimize various processes, ranging from storage and transportation to quality control. This technology allows for real-time data collection, analysis, and decision-making, ensuring that food products meet the highest safety and quality standards.

Lastly, the field of chemical engineering plays a crucial role in developing sustainable packaging solutions. As the world becomes increasingly aware of the environmental impact of single-use plastics, researchers are exploring alternative materials and techniques. Bio-based polymers, compostable packaging, and edible coatings are just a few examples of innovations that are reducing waste and promoting a circular economy.

In conclusion, emerging technologies and innovations in food engineering are shaping the future of the industry. From sustainable farming practices to advanced processing techniques and smart packaging solutions, these advancements are improving the quality, safety, and sustainability of our food. As consumers, it is essential to stay informed about these developments and support the adoption of technologies that align with our values of health, sustainability, and innovation.

Industry 4.0: Digitalization and Automation in Food Manufacturing

In this digital age, the food manufacturing industry is undergoing a transformative shift towards Industry 4.0. Technology advancements such as digitalization and automation are revolutionizing the way food products are designed, produced, and distributed. This subchapter explores the impact of these technologies on the food manufacturing sector, with a focus on their relevance to chemical engineering professionals.

Digitalization, the process of integrating digital technologies into various aspects of production, has significantly enhanced efficiency and productivity in the food manufacturing industry. From data analytics to artificial intelligence, digital tools are enabling manufacturers to optimize their processes, reduce waste, and improve product quality. Chemical engineers, in particular, play a crucial role in leveraging digitalization to streamline manufacturing operations. They can utilize data-driven insights to optimize ingredient formulations, improve process efficiency, and enhance product consistency. By harnessing the power of digitalization, chemical engineers can contribute to the development of innovative and sustainable food products.

Automation is another key component of Industry 4.0 that is reshaping food manufacturing. The use of robotics and automated systems has revolutionized the production line, making it faster, more accurate, and less labor-intensive. Chemical engineers with expertise in process control and optimization can design and implement automated systems that ensure precise ingredient dosing, efficient mixing, and accurate packaging. By automating repetitive tasks, food manufacturers can minimize human errors, increase production capacity, and achieve consistent product quality.

Furthermore, digitalization and automation have opened up new opportunities for customization and personalization in food manufacturing. With the help of advanced technologies, manufacturers can cater to individual consumer preferences, dietary restrictions, and nutritional requirements. Chemical engineers can leverage their expertise in formulation and process optimization to develop customized food products that meet these specific needs. This trend towards personalized nutrition has the potential to revolutionize the food industry, allowing for a more targeted and consumer-centric approach to product development.

In conclusion, the integration of digitalization and automation in food manufacturing is transforming the industry and offering exciting opportunities for chemical engineering professionals. By embracing these technologies, manufacturers can enhance their efficiency, improve product quality, and meet evolving consumer demands. Chemical engineers, equipped with their knowledge of process optimization and formulation, are well-positioned to drive innovation in this digital era of food product design.

Challenges and Opportunities in Food Engineering

Food engineering is a field that combines the principles of chemical engineering with the intricacies of the food industry. It plays a vital role in the development and production of safe, nutritious, and sustainable food products. However, like any other field, food engineering also faces its fair share of challenges and opportunities. In this subchapter, we will explore some of the key challenges and exciting prospects that lie ahead in the world of food engineering.

One of the foremost challenges in food engineering is ensuring food safety. With an ever-increasing global population and complex supply chains, it is imperative to develop robust systems that can prevent contamination and ensure the integrity of food products. Chemical engineers play a crucial role in developing novel techniques for food preservation, sterilization, and packaging, thereby minimizing the risk of foodborne illnesses.

Another significant challenge is the development of sustainable food processes. As the world grapples with issues such as climate change and depleting resources, it is crucial to find innovative ways to reduce energy consumption, minimize waste generation, and optimize production processes. Chemical engineers can contribute by devising environmentally-friendly technologies, such as energy-efficient drying methods or waste valorization processes.

Furthermore, the field of food engineering presents exciting opportunities for innovation and product development. With the ever-changing consumer preferences and demands, there is a constant need to create new and improved food products. Chemical engineers can leverage their expertise in areas such as formulation, flavor encapsulation, and texture modification to create healthier, tastier, and more sustainable food options.

Additionally, advancements in technology, such as artificial intelligence and big data analytics, present new avenues for optimizing food processes and improving product quality. By harnessing these technologies, food engineers can enhance efficiency, reduce costs, and deliver personalized food experiences to consumers.

For those pursuing a career in chemical engineering, specializing in food engineering offers a unique set of challenges and opportunities. It combines the principles of chemical engineering with the intricacies of the food industry, allowing individuals to make a tangible impact on global food security, public health, and sustainability.

In conclusion, the field of food engineering is rife with challenges and opportunities. From ensuring food safety to developing sustainable processes and innovating new food products, chemical engineers have a crucial role to play. By embracing these challenges and seeking out opportunities for innovation, individuals can contribute to the advancement of food engineering and make a positive impact on the world of food.

Chapter 11: Conclusion

Recapitulation of Key Concepts

In this subchapter, we will take a moment to summarize the key concepts that we have explored throughout the book, "Mastering Food Product Design: A Journey into the World of Food Engineering." Whether you are a student of chemical engineering or simply someone interested in the world of food, this recapitulation aims to provide a comprehensive overview of the fundamental ideas covered.

1. Food Engineering: We began by establishing the importance of food engineering and its role in designing innovative and safe food products. This interdisciplinary field combines principles from chemical engineering, microbiology, nutrition, and sensory science to create food products that meet consumer demands.

2. Food Product Design Process: We then delved into the food product design process, which involves defining product objectives, conducting market research, generating ideas, prototyping, and finally, commercialization. Understanding this process is vital for successfully developing new food products that cater to consumer needs.

3. Food Safety and Quality: Ensuring food safety and quality is of utmost importance in the food industry. We explored various aspects such as hazard analysis, critical control points, Good Manufacturing Practices (GMP), and quality control measures to maintain the highest standards in food production.

4. Ingredient Selection and Functionality: The choice and functionality of ingredients play a crucial role in food product design. We discussed the properties and functionalities of key ingredients such as

carbohydrates, proteins, lipids, and additives, along with their impact on product texture, flavor, and shelf life.

5. Food Processing Techniques: An understanding of different food processing techniques is essential for transforming raw ingredients into finished food products. We covered topics like thermal processing, drying, freezing, and packaging, highlighting their effects on product safety, quality, and stability.

6. Sensory Evaluation: Sensory evaluation allows us to understand consumer preferences and perceptions of food products. We explored various sensory testing methods, including taste panels, consumer surveys, and instrumental analysis, to evaluate attributes such as taste, texture, aroma, and appearance.

7. Sustainability in Food Engineering: Lastly, we emphasized the importance of sustainability in food engineering. As chemical engineers, we have a responsibility to develop environmentally friendly and resource-efficient processes that minimize waste and energy consumption.

By revisiting these key concepts, we hope to reinforce your understanding of food product design and inspire you to apply these principles in your own endeavors. Whether you aspire to be a food engineer or simply wish to enhance your knowledge of the subject, "Mastering Food Product Design: A Journey into the World of Food Engineering" equips you with the essential tools to excel in the captivating realm of food engineering.

Inspiring the Next Generation of Food Engineers

As the world's population continues to grow, so does the demand for safe, nutritious, and sustainable food. This growing need has created an exciting opportunity for young minds to explore the field of food engineering and play an integral role in shaping the future of food production. In this subchapter, we aim to inspire and educate individuals from all walks of life about the vast potential and importance of food engineering, particularly for those interested in the niche of Chemical Engineering.

Food engineering combines principles from various disciplines such as chemistry, biology, and engineering to develop innovative and efficient processes for producing, processing, and packaging food products. It encompasses a wide range of areas, including food preservation, nutraceuticals, flavor enhancement, and food safety. By mastering food product design, engineers can create healthier, tastier, and more sustainable food options to meet the ever-evolving needs of consumers.

For those with a background or interest in Chemical Engineering, the field of food engineering offers an exciting opportunity to apply their knowledge and skills to tackle complex challenges. Chemical engineers possess a deep understanding of thermodynamics, mass transfer, and reaction kinetics, which are fundamental in designing and optimizing food processes. By leveraging their expertise, these engineers can contribute to developing novel techniques for food production, such as microencapsulation for controlled release of nutrients or designing bioreactors to cultivate alternative protein sources.

Furthermore, food engineering offers a unique blend of creativity and technical expertise. It requires individuals to think outside the box and come up with innovative solutions to improve food quality, extend shelf life, and reduce waste. From creating sustainable packaging materials to developing novel extraction methods, the possibilities are endless. By inspiring the next generation of food engineers, we can harness their creativity and passion to drive meaningful advancements in the food industry.

To nurture this passion, it is vital to provide aspiring food engineers with the necessary education and resources. Universities and educational institutions should offer specialized food engineering programs or include food-related courses in their curriculum. Additionally, industry collaborations and internships can provide hands-on experience and expose students to real-world challenges.

In conclusion, inspiring the next generation of food engineers is crucial to meet the increasing global demand for safe and sustainable food. For those with a background in Chemical Engineering, the field of food engineering offers an exciting avenue to apply their skills and contribute to the future of food production. By fostering creativity, providing education, and encouraging industry collaborations, we can empower individuals to embark on a fulfilling journey into the world of food engineering.

Printed in the USA
CPSIA information can be obtained
at www.ICGtesting.com
LVHW010836070324
773597LV00015B/709